FOREWORD

Much of my success as a professional quilter and designer stems from my desire to create a home filled with calm, quiet, and comfort—but most of all love. For many years I've focused my creative energies on making my family the center of our home. Along the way I've had the privilege of being a source of inspiration for many others seeking the same satisfaction gained from making a house a home.

It is my sincere hope that through the pages of this book you'll discover for yourself how easy it is to celebrate the seasons with simple country accents for every room of your house. After all, what can be more rewarding than sharing many of your favorite things with all of your favorite people? If making harmony the heart of your home is as important to you as it is to me, then *Classic Country* is meant just for you!

Lynette Jensen

THIMBLEBERRIES®

Classic Country

by
Lynette Jensen

Four Seasons of Lifestyle, Decorating,
Entertaining & Quilting Inspirations

Copyright© 2002 by Landauer Corporation

Projects Copyright© 2002 by Lynette Jensen

This book was designed, produced, and published by Landauer Books
A division of Landauer Corporation
12251 Maffitt Road, Cumming, Iowa 50061

President: Jeramy Lanigan Landauer
Vice President: Becky Johnston
Art Director: Laurel Albright
Creative Director: Lynette Jensen
Photographers: Craig Anderson, Amy Cooper, and Dennis Kennedy
Photostyling: Lynette Jensen and Margaret Sindelar
Technical Writer: Sue Bahr
Technical Illustrator: Lisa Kirchoff

We also wish to thank the support staff of the Thimbleberries® Design Studio:
Sherry Husske, Virginia Brodd, Renae Ashwill, Ardelle Paulson, Kathy Lobeck,
Carla Plowman, Julie Jergens, Pearl Baysinger, Tracy Schrantz, Leone Rusch, and Julie Borg.
Also, Suzanne Maki for decorative painting and Sue Graff for window treatments.

This book is printed on acid-free paper.

Printed in China 10 9 8 7 6 5 4 3 2 1

ISBN: 1-890621-43-9

Contents

INTRODUCTION

For best-selling quilting author and fabric designer, Lynette Jensen, all the comforts of home are found in this lovingly restored two-story Colonial she shares with her husband Neil and two grown children, Matthew and Kerry, who visit regularly.

Through the pages of this book, Lynette shares her secrets for successful classic country decorating through a personal tour of her home and gardens. She will show you how to quickly mix and match colors, blend decorating styles, and highlight favorite family pieces through a simple planning process that takes you from basic to beautiful in a matter of minutes.

Discover how easy it is to create a sense of well-being throughout your home with four seasons of classic country decorating themes inspired by designer and teacher Lynette Jensen's unique gift for making harmony the heart of the home.

Collecting

Lynette's passion for collecting began when she couldn't bear to see precious pieces of the past tossed out to make room for the new. Since beauty is in the eye of the beholder, it wasn't long before other people's trash became her treasures.

As a frequent flyer through neighborhood garage sales and antique shops, Lynette hauled home other people's castoffs, many of which have now become collectibles in their own right.

Featured below are paper and fabric quilt patterns in miniature or scraps of vintage textiles such as a crazy quilt in a variety of antique frames. Cross-stitched samplers or crewel embroidery all depicting a similar theme such as a cottage are grouped for greater impact. Fragile antique paper items such as vintage paper dolls can be a challenge to preserve and yet display—framing easily solves the problem.

Quilting

The transition from salvaging scraps of vintage textiles and tattered quilts to collecting quality heirlooms was gradual, but became more affordable when Lynette's husband completed law school at the University of Minnesota. After Neil Jensen's graduation, they settled in his hometown of Hutchinson, Minnesota, to establish the law practice which he still maintains. Lynette found herself busy with two small children, yet eager to fulfill her creative interests. One day quite by accident she attended a show in a nearby rural community featuring a wonderful display of quilts and antiques gathered by a local quilt collector.

Lynette can still recall thinking to herself, "This is exactly what I want to do."

Soon Lynette was not only collecting quilts, but making them for every room of her house.

Whether antique or recently handcrafted, Lynette finds creative ways to display every new addition to her ever-growing collection of quilts. For a great mix of colors in almost any room, quilts are folded and tucked everywhere—in cupboards and on shelves, in a large antique box from a fish market; in a small wooden tool caddy; and in a much larger old wooden tool box parked on a bench housing even more quilts and comforters.

Designing Fabric

Expressing her creativity through quilting, Lynette discovered that by designing her own line of coordinating prints, solids, and plaids she could get exactly what she needed for her growing collection of pieced patchwork. A licensing agreement signed with RJR Fashion Fabrics in 1993 has resulted in an expansive line of fabrics anchored by her signature Paintbox Collection.

Known and respected through the quilting world for her Thimbleberries® line of fabrics, Lynette has created an enduring collection of coordinates in a rich palette of country colors that literally spans the seasons. Lynette combines traditional quilt patterns with an appealing array of appliquéd vines, berries, and blossoms. The result is a charming blend of blocks and borders with soft touches of country color for a unique style reminiscent of America's more tranquil past.

Lynette's fabric designs have so much appeal that her design studio located in downtown Hutchinson, in a 100-year-old building with original tin ceilings and hardwood floors has become a destination for Thimbleberries® enthusiasts who visit from around the world. Main Street Cotton Shop, an independent full-service quilting shop located in the Thimbleberries® building, currently stocks the entire line of Thimbleberries® patterns, books, fabrics, and quilts.

For Lynette, a Minnesota native and graduate of the University of Minnesota in Home Economics, the Thimbleberries® design studio and office is a short walk from the home she shares with husband Neil. The spacious studio, filled with antiques and quilts on display, is a wonderful, open, bright spot from which to work and create each day.

Living a Dream

For Lynette, the true joy of her business is that designing quilts and fabric involves doing exactly what she would choose to do for a hobby.

The company she started in 1989 with the introduction of four quilt patterns by now features more than 70 patterns, 20 softcover books, as well as 3 hardcover books published by Rodale Press.

Thimbleberries® also offers regular new fabric collections, block-of-the month quilt patterns, and a popular club conducted by quilt shops internationally.

Lynette has been a featured guest on television quilting programs and featured in leading publications such as *American Patchwork & Quilting* and *McCall's Quilting*.

Thimbleberries® exhibits Lynette's new collections twice yearly at the International Quilt Market. As her design schedule permits, throughout the year Lynette conducts workshops and lectures both nationally and internationally.

However, her home and heart are solidly in Hutchinson, Minnesota, where even when relaxing in the backyard, Lynette shares her enthusiasm for classic country decorating with family, friends, and business associates alike.

Spring

Summer

Harvest

Holiday

OVERVIEW

With today's lifestyles calling for home decorating
ideas, make your house a home with special, personal touches
you add yourself. As you greet each new season
of the year, treat your family and friends to four seasons
of fresh new lifestyle, decorating, entertaining and
quilting inspirations from Lynette Jensen.

On the following pages, you'll find a chapter devoted to
each season—spring, summer, harvest, and holiday—filled
with recipes, ideas, and projects for surface design, home decor,
woodpainting, stenciling, and fun with fabric. Step-by-step
how-tos, illustrations, and full-size patterns, along with a
complete guide to materials and sources, provide a hands-on
guide to creating it yourself.

Lynette has also included a special section of "swatches to
go"—coordinating fabric and color chips created especially for
each season that blend perfectly to transition you through the
year in style. Thanks to Lynette, you can make it beautiful and
make it easy, too. From decorating to entertaining, Lynette
Jensen offers you the best of everything for creating four seasons
of your own authentic country lifestyle!

Spring Haven

"For me, spring seems to be the first season of the year—filled with new beginnings and the promise of even greater things to come."

For Lynette, spring is the first season of the year and, the garage is the first room of the house. With her busy lifestyle, it occurred to Lynette that on a daily basis she saw more of her garage than she did many of the rooms of her house.

Determined to make the garage a place of welcome, Lynette cleaned out all the clutter and painted the walls. Using a combination of several commercial stencils, Lynette topped each wall with a floral stenciled border which immediately lifted the mood to make the garage more cheery than dreary.

Lynette then created a convenient potting center by filling a corner of the garage with an old jelly cupboard crowned with a gate from her grandmother's garden where Lynette recalls spending many pleasant hours as a child. Other keepsakes that bring back happy memories include the well-worn garden hat and sprinkling can that belonged to her grandmother along with the washboard and garden spade used so often by her mother.

In creating the potting center, Lynette found it unnecessary to replace the glass in the doors of the jelly cupboard because none of the contents—a hodgepodge of ceramic pots, pails, and pans—needed to be kept dust-free. With her assorted garden tools handy, Lynette finds it easy to "think spring" even during Minnesota's harsh winters. Everything she needs to get a head start on seedlings for planting her spring haven is gathered in a memory-filled corner of her garage—a unique "welcome home" center!

"Thinking spring" may be as easy as filling a cupboard with bowls and plates looking much like buds and blooms. Or for a "hearty" springtime welcome, fill the front hall table with stenciled boxes brimming with old-fashioned homemade caramels for friends and family to enjoy.

Recipe

Old-Fashioned Caramels

1 cup butter

2 1/4 cups firmly packed brown sugar

1 cup light corn syrup

14 oz. can sweetened condensed milk

1 1/2 teaspoons vanilla

4" squares of waxed paper

Buttered 9"-square pan

In a heavy 3 quart saucepan, melt butter. Add sugar and mix until well blended. Stir in corn syrup; cook until sugar has dissolved; remove pan from heat. Stir in sweetened condensed milk; cook over medium heat, stirring constantly until mixture reaches the soft ball stage (240°), about 20–30 minutes. Add vanilla. Pour hot mixture into prepared pan. Cool. Use spatula to remove from pan. Cut 36 caramels; wrap individually in waxed paper.

Spring is often a season of small beginnings with big results. Lynette challenged members of her quilt guild by giving each a pattern and a bag of fabric scraps. One of the resulting quilts was The Homespun Stars wall quilt shown, opposite. It was so stunning Lynette had to have it! (See page 112 for instructions.)

Lynette's "Beaner" Bunnies greet spring in vests made from fabric scraps. (See page 114 for instructions.) Here, quilts in glorious shades of pastels are like a field of spring flowers all bursting into bloom at once.

Papier-maché bunnies from flea markets can tote more than candy. Beginning in early spring, Lynette fills them with fresh flowers or with painted eggs nestled on Easter basket grass. The tiny yellow chicks, below, were always on the kitchen window sill when Lynette was a child.

Lynette welcomes spring with painted wooden eggs guaranteed to last the season. With help from her daughter, Kerry, Lynette colors eggs in anticipation of Sunday morning brunch.

Spring Table Favors

Sandwich together chick-shaped sugar cookies (see page 100 for recipe) using powdered sugar frosting with a bamboo skewer between the two cookies. When frosting has hardened, insert skewer into flower oasis that has been fitted into a small flower pot. Insert various lengths of artificial bear grass (can be purchased at a floral shop), into the oasis surrounding the cookie. Add a ribbon bow if desired. Nestle the flower pot in a dish of gumdrops for soft pastel color.

Fruit Compote

1 can cherry pie filling

1 15-oz. can pineapple chunks, with juice

1 8-oz. pkg. pitted prunes

Mix all 3 ingredients. Bake at 350° for 1 hour. Serve warm. Serves 10–12.

Grilled Cinnamon Rolls

Purchase cinnamon rolls from your favorite bakery and cut each roll in half horizontally. Butter each half. Grill in a frying pan on medium heat until golden brown. Cover with foil until ready to serve.

Parmesan Potatoes

2 lbs. shredded potatoes

1/2 cup melted butter

2 cups half- and-half cream

4 oz. grated parmesan cheese

4 oz. shredded cheddar cheese

Mix all ingredients together in order given and place in a greased 9" x 13" pan. Bake at 350° for 1–1/2 hours. Serves 10–12.

Egg Sausage Bake

8 eggs, slightly beaten

6 slices bread, cubed

2 cups milk

1 cup shredded cheddar cheese

1 teaspoon dry mustard

1 teaspoon salt

1/4 teaspoon pepper

16 oz. bulk breakfast sausage, cooked and drained

Mix all ingredients. Place in a greased 9" x 13" pan; refrigerate overnight. Bake at 350° for 35 minutes. Serves 8–10.

In the spring, rabbits have a way of multiplying rapidly—almost as fast as Lynette's ever-growing collection of those same charming creatures!

Filling every nook and cranny is always a collector's dream, and Lynette found the challenge of the typical "too narrow to do anything with" space at the top of the stairs just that. She discovered that an antique child's cupboard was just the right size and width to fill the space, but not block the entrance to the adjoining bedroom. Resisting the temptation to give the cupboard a spring spruce up, Lynette left the original paint

and bunny decals. Previously referred to as "peeling paint," now those same features are quite popular in their own right. Crackle glazes and finishes are purposely added to new pieces to make them look old and weathered.

As part of her decorating philosophy, Lynette Jensen is convinced that "what goes around comes around,"

and is content to just let old pieces "be."

Faded papier-maché bunnies from one era seem right at home with newly-purchased pastel pottery flower pots and antique vases.

To create a charming spring decorating theme, Lynette finds it best to group lots of one kind of accessory like the bunnies shown here. She ties them all together with a unifying theme such as the wooden, papier-maché, and candy eggs scattered about just as if the Easter Bunny had already come and gone early on a Sunday morning!

Kerry's room, shown here
in full bloom, is a sample
of lots of spring "stuff"
(as Lynette fondly refers
to it all), successfully
sharing the same small space.

The room's centerpiece is
the Courtyard Garden quilt
Lynette designed combined with
her Poppies and Cottage Flower
quilt patterns. Other accents
include Lynette's crocheted rug,
pottery, and papier-maché
boxes covered with old
magazine finds such as
Dolly Dingle paper-doll cutouts.

Details in Kerry's bedroom include an appliquéd floral vine Lynette designed for a pillow cover. (See page 116 for instructions.) Lynette brings more of the outdoors in with an old garden gate perched on a dresser. A framed *Good Housekeeping* cover features a girl playing tennis—her daughter's sport throughout her school years.

"The dime-sized hexagons in this antique Grandmother's Flower Garden quilt with crocheted picot edging make it unique."

"A vintage paper doll with the same spelling of my daughter's name, complete with outfits and a kitty was quite a find."

Decoupage

Papier-maché box with lid

Latex wall paint

Modge Podge Glue®

Paper dolls or other paper shapes

Step 1   Paint the papier-maché box and lid with any color latex paint you like. Let dry for 4 hours.

Step 2   Cut out the paper dolls or other paper shapes to be used on the box.

Step 3   Cover the box and the lid with Modge Podge®. While the glue is still wet, position the cut-out shapes on the box and lid, being careful to have the shapes positioned below the overlap of the lid. Let dry for 4 hours.

Step 4   To seal the surface of the box and paper cut-outs, cover the box and the lid once again with Modge Podge®. Let dry for 4 hours.

The rag balls shown here have been passed on to Lynette from the supply her grandmother had ready for rug weaving whenever she had a spare moment. Lynette learned rugmaking from a dear friend and uses a rug hook carved by her friend's husband. (See page 118 for instructions.)

"I learned to sew on my grandmother's treadle sewing machine— sewing strips of fabric together for rug rag balls just like these."

Lynette designed The Flower Bed quilt shown on the previous page as a continuing tribute to her love for flower beds filled with spring flowers.

(See page 119 for instructions.)

In this small guest bedroom, more of Lynette's love for spring's new beginnings is evident in the embroidered chicks soaking up the sun on the blocks featured in her Flowers in Bloom quilt and matching Baby Chicks pillow.

The guest room shown here and on the previous pages is bursting with flowers— from framed to fresh! Blending the old with the new is Lynette's specialty. Her childhood tea set nestled in the tiny cupboard tops off a collection of other favorite toys kept and waiting for playtime to begin.

"This antique block was carefully saved from Neil's parents' wedding quilt and preserved under glass."

Summer Hideaway

"Indoors or out, creating a special summer hideaway often requires more imagination than money."

Lynette believes that indoors or out, creating a special summer hideaway often requires more imagination than money.

She leads the way in this porch filled with an eclectic mix of old and older, all costing much less than if purchased new. For instance, Lynette counts the table in the foreground as one of the best garage-sale buys to date.

A friend who is also an experienced garage-sale shopper found this table and at first glance it was so beat up that even she failed to take notice. However, on thinking it over she decided to go back the next day and see if this diamond- in- the-

rough was still available for the magnificent sum of 25 cents. To her delight, remaining items from the sale had been marked down to half price. She took the table home for 12-1/2 cents!

Lynette now counts it as one of the all-time favorite gifts she has received.

Feeling like she couldn't mess the table up anymore,

Lynette experimented with coats of paint and a sailboat stencil inspired by glasses passed down to her from her grandmother Halverson.

Other oldies but goodies include the tin lunch pails, wicker picnic baskets, and toy tops and drum.

Project

Sailboat Table

Paint table with a light color such as beige latex paint. Paint table with a second coat of medium-blue latex paint.

Let dry overnight and sand lightly with medium-grain sand paper to reveal some of the lighter color underneath. On edges that would show wear on a vintage piece, sand off some of both coats revealing raw wood.

Stencil boat and star design as desired.

With a rag, apply a coat of medium stain and wipe off excess immediately. The stain will give the table finish a little patina and will settle the stencil into the surface.

Allow to dry completely. To protect from wear and moisture apply a coat of matte finish polyurethane.

Project

Lamp Shade Trim

Measure circumference of lamp shade both at the top and bottom. Add 2" to each measurement.

Cut 2 bias strips 1-1/2" wide by the length of above measurements.

Press each strip in half lengthwise creasing slightly.

Unfold and press each lengthwise raw edge to center fold.

Apply white fabric glue to bottom edge of lamp shade applying a narrow line of glue around the shade edge.

Align fabric binding on right side of shade with center fold on edge of shade.

To finish and cover raw edge of binding end, fold under end of bias strip and overlap raw end of bias strip. Extra glue needs to be applied at this point to secure.

Apply another line of glue on the inside edge of the shade and fold bias strip to inside of shade pressing firmly to glued edge.

Repeat for top edge trim of the lamp shade.

"The best summer
hideaway I can imagine
is filled with things
made by hand—
from the crocheted rug on
the floor to the Midnight
Sky quilt complete
with shining stars."

"I love to buy the most
inexpensive and boring
lamp I can find and then
give it some real
personality by stenciling
summer flowers on the base
and adding a country-plaid
binding to the shade."

Assemble the Inner Pillowcase

Step 1 To make the hem on the RED PRINT fabric, turn one long edge under 1", and press. Turn the same edge under 1" again and press. Topstitch in place to finish the pillowcase hem.

Step 2 With right sides together, fold the hemmed rectangle in half and sew the raw edges together using a 1/4" seam allowance. Turn the pillowcase right side out. Insert the pillowform, and hand-stitch the opening closed.

Fold

Assemble the Outer Pillowcase

Step 1 Hem the 20-1/2" x 36-1/2" RED PLAID rectangle in the same manner as for the inner pillowcase.

Step 2 Repeat Step 2 as for the inner pillowcase, but do not insert the pillow form or hand-stitch the opening closed.

Step 3 To make each of the ties, fold one short end of a 3" x 18-1/2" RED PLAID strip under 1/4", and press. Fold the long edges under to meet at the center.

Step 4 Fold the strip in half lengthwise again, and stitch 1/8" away from the folded edges. At this point the tie should measure 3/4" x 18-1/2".

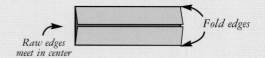

Fold edges

Raw edges meet in center

Step 5 Insert the raw edges of the ties 1-1/4" to the inside of each side of the opening of the outer pillowcase, taking care to space them evenly. Stitch the ties in place along the edges of the pillowcase and through the hem.

Folded edges

Step 6 Insert the inner pillow into the outer pillowcase, and tie each of the ties in a bow.

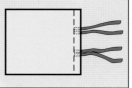

Project

Porch Pillow with Ties

18" square

Yardage is based on 42" wide fabric

Fabrics and Supplies (for 1 pillow)
- 2/3 yard RED PRINT fabric for inner pillowcase
- 1 yard RED PLAID fabric for outer pillowcase
- 18" square pillow form

(Before beginning this project, read through General Instructions on page 110.)

Cutting

From the RED PRINT:
- Cut 1, 20-1/2" x 36-1/2" rectangle for inner pillowcase

From the RED PLAID:
- Cut 1, 20-1/2" x 36-1/2" rectangle for outer pillowcase
- Cut 4, 3" x 18-1/2" strips for ties

Watering cans, bird houses, picnic baskets, and Fourth of July flags are sure signs of summer, and what retreat would be complete without a few of these old favorites? Lynette aptly demonstrates how festive red, white, and green can transcend the seasons for a rousing salute to summer!

"The pillow cover with ties is appropriately casual for the porch setting, revealing a touch of contrasting color."

"Regardless of its size, the master bedroom should be the one place filled with keepsakes that belong just to you."

For true rest and relaxation, Lynette feels strongly that the master bedroom should serve the purpose of all private places and spaces—it must be a reflection of your true tastes and interests.

In Lynette's special summer hideaway that means surrounding herself with treasures that money can't buy such as the floral embroidered pillowcases made by a special friend, the handsome pillow front embroidered by her mother many years ago, an antique appliquéd quilt, and the collection of framed quilt patterns in miniature grouped above the bed.

Transforming an ordinary room into an extraordinary retreat often means seeking subtle ways to encourage solitude and serenity without sacrificing modern conveniences such as morning news and talk shows on television. Lynette discovered an easy way to accomplish that was to have a red-roofed house specially built to accommodate the TV—with doors that are almost always closed when Lynette is in residence! Lynette finds that keeping clutter out of sight also keeps it out of mind as a further inducement to restful thinking and relaxing.

Numerous stenciled boxes provide storage for small items such as cards and photos that might otherwise create clutter. Keeping it all under cover also means bringing in trunks and baskets to hold extra pillows, blankets, and a quilt or two. Many of the blocks and borders Lynette chooses for her quilts blend with simple stencil patterns that grace the walls and windows.

The master bedroom can be the perfect hideaway for a retreat at the end of a long day. Lynette makes it an inviting place to curl up with a book or watch a movie on the television cleverly hidden inside the little red-roofed house.

"Adding a generous ruffle to pillowcases allows them to blend gracefully with the quilt and matching bedskirt."

Stenciled Walls

All supplies are available from hobby or craft stores.

Latex wall paint

Template plastic
(if you are cutting your own stencils)
or
Variety of purchased stencils

Stencil paints

Stencil brushes

Stenciling

Step 1   Paint walls a neutral color. Rag or sponge a slightly lighter color for added interest.

Step 2   Using the stencil paints, stencil the shapes on the wall. Work with a very small amount of paint on the stencil brush, pounding the brush lightly to apply the paint. Apply paint at the edges of the cut-out, working toward the center. The variation of color between the lighter and darker areas enhances the hand-painted effect.

As often as possible, Lynette tries to incorporate a house into the decorating theme. Here, a doll house used as a towel caddy sits snugly along one wall of the upstairs bathroom. Vertical stenciling creates a wallpaper effect for framed threadwork kittens and a summertime watercolor scene dated 1939.

"Stenciling is an old art with new uses—It's fun to discover how much surface you can cover with so little paint!"

Coordinating a Collection

"Before recovering your furniture or investing in new upholstered pieces, an easy way to see if a coordinating collection of stripes, prints, plaids, and solids really work well together is to combine the fabrics randomly on the fronts and backs of pillows for the patio. Stitch up a stack of over-sized pillows to mix and match and you'll soon discover your favorite combination."

"Park your plants on an old shutter and the slant of the slats will easily allow for drainage and proper air circulation."

At sunset, small pails painted and stenciled are home to citronella candles which ward off pesky mosquitoes while providing a romantic glow.

> *"Treat yourself to a slice of summer by creating a backyard hideaway complete with a picket fence."*

Lynette shows you how to treat yourself to a slice of summer by creating a backyard hideaway complete with the proverbial white picket fence—in portable sections to move around as desired! To make your own fence, use varying lengths of 1"- x 3"-wide pine nailed to two cross pieces of 1" x 2" pine to make sections. Hinge sections of the fence, and use it anywhere.

Use the charming watermelon motif for appliqués on chair backs and as a stencil for coordinating everything from trays to canning jar vases. (See page 122 for instructions.)

The chair-back covers with ties are particularly easy to make and dress up ordinary folding chairs. For the ruffle and the pink watermelon, Lynette chose a pink plaid fabric that coordinates with the plaid fabric used for the tablecloth. The pink plaid is also paired with a small-print fabric for the double-faced napkin.

Additional watermelon accents include the stenciled serving tray and canning jar vases, citronella candle pails, painted and stenciled tubs stacked to create a clever ice bucket for chilled beverages, and inexpensive plates and bowls.

For the place mats, first stencil the watermelon motif, and then add floral borders using purchased stencils for added interest.

Lynette complements the decorating theme with a menu featuring Rhubarb Punch and Watermelon Romaine Salad. For these light and refreshing recipes, please turn the page.

Watermelon Romaine Salad

2 heads of romaine lettuce, washed, dried and torn into pieces

2 tablespoons of sesame seeds

2 cups cubed watermelon with seeds removed

1 red onion, peeled, quartered and thinly sliced

Dressing (below)

Toast sesame seeds on pie plate in preheated 350° oven until golden, approximately 10 minutes. Set aside.

Toss romaine, onions, and dressing together. Top with melon cubes and sesame seeds. Serves 6.

Substitute strawberries, pears, kiwi or pomegranate seeds for the melon.

Dressing

1/4 cup safflower oil

2 tablespoons high quality balsamic vinegar

2-1/2 tablespoons sugar

1 teaspoon salt

Dash of pepper

Dash of Tobasco sauce

Place all ingredients in blender and blend to dissolve sugar. Refrigerate.

Rhubarb Punch

12 cups rhubarb, sliced

6 quarts water

1 6-oz. can frozen orange juice (undiluted)

1 12-oz. can frozen lemonade (undiluted)

3 cups sugar (this may be cut back to 2 cups for a punch that is not quite as sweet)

1 quart 7-Up® or club soda (again, club soda would not be quite as sweet, but very refreshing)

Boil the rhubarb and water together until rhubarb is very soft and falls apart. Strain. Add the orange juice, lemonade, and sugar to the strained liquid; mix together until the sugar is dissolved. Add soda just before serving. Serves 8–10.

Several years ago Lynette and Neil Jensen welcomed the once-in-a-lifetime opportunity to purchase their two-story Colonial nestled in a neighborhood filled with historic houses. The house offered Lynette the opportunity to restore another old house and establish numerous flower gardens.

As an added incentive, the house was majestically situated on a hill overlooking the bend of a river. The backyard has become a cherished hideaway offering a commanding view of the Crow River which meanders gently through their small town.

Harvest Homecoming

Autumn comes early to Minnesota and Lynette thoroughly enjoys the golden hues of the last leaves of summer lingering on the towering trees surrounding her home.

For the backyard, Lynette designed a series of stone retaining walls which provide ample growing space for a cascading series of plantings including perennials such as Cranesbill Blue Geraniums and Autumn Joy Sedum. Here, Lynette gathers an assortment of autumn's finest for a dried floral bouquet to complement a treasured family quilt believed to be more than 100 years old.

Project

Pumpkin Presentation

"Display gourd-pumpkin jack-o-lanterns on a trellis of Morning Glory vine and leaves. Here, an iron plant cage serves as a basket for pumpkins and gourds. It is the perfect height for elevating the vibrant orange of the pumpkins to mix with evergreens and fall flowers."

Tuck pumpkins in among flowering plants and evergreens— bringing fall color to parts of the garden that ordinarily no longer have colorful blooms.

"Several years ago I discovered white pumpkins and asked a local farmer to grow them for me. They have since become quite popular and add nice contrast to the landscape!"

Pumpkins, real and imagined (on Lynette's Harvest Time quilt), abound in displays throughout the house at harvest time. Lynette selects pumpkins of all shapes and sizes and then chooses a palette of warm country colors ranging from toasty browns to deep shades of goldenrod.

"Visitors are often surprised to discover that this relic given to me by my Dad was a milk-can cart."

In the family room, an antique toy barn takes center stage on an old chest of drawers nestled under the window next to the fireplace. Wanting to let in as much light as possible, Lynette opted for a simple window treatment and created the

mock double ruffle on the window valance out of sheer necessity. In her fabric stash Lynette had plenty of the striped fabric but only a scrap of the wheat-colored linen. Adding a few inches of it to the top and bottom of the striped yardage (from the back) created the illusion of a full-length ruffle.

Lynette's palette of warm country colors ranging from toasty browns to deep shades of goldenrod are just as effective in her collection of pottery as in her fabric choices. Another accent that brings the harvest theme indoors is the framed wool appliqué pumpkin project. (See page 126 for instructions.)

"Many of my quilt block designs such as the Heart Blossom Five-Patch quilt draped over the chair, are harvest inspired."

Paired with an antique wooden bowl, freshly painted papier-maché pumpkins are crackle-finished to look old. Lynette enjoys the challenge of finding ways to transform an entire room such as the kitchen with seasonal accents in a matter of minutes.

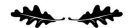

Prime examples of her quick-change artistry are kitchen towels accented with sunflower and pumpkin motifs. By using light and dark shades of fabrics, Lynette creates the illusion of several different pumpkins from one simple pattern.

(See page 124 for instructions.)

Gracing the sideboard in the dining room, Lynette's handsome Pumpkins for Sale wall quilt is surrounded by symbols of the harvest season— a sunflower, pumpkin, and a handful of autumn leaves.

(See page 127 for instructions.)

"For a country-harvest of color, I combine quilts with collectibles—everything from a child's chalkboard to antique stitcheries."

Project

Drying Flowers

"Over the years I have found that the easiest way to dry most flowers is to pick them when they are at their peak. Hang them upside down in a dry location away from direct sunlight. For hydrangeas, pick them in late summer, just as they dry on the plant. When they feel like parchment paper they are ready to cut."

Every autumn, Lynette

anticipates a full harvest of

her own homegrown

hydrangeas to add color,

texture, and volume to

dried floral arrangements.

Lynette's Harvest

Pinwheels quilt is the

perfect color complement

to an antique plant

stand brimming with

dried blooms. (See page

131 for instructions.)

"Keeping the cookie jar filled with homemade cookies is a constant challenge, but a joy as well."

Keeping the cookie jar filled with homemade cookies is a constant challenge for Lynette when son, Matt, comes home to visit (and snack!).

"My mother gave us the old green jar when Neil and I moved into our first house.

"Over the years I've tried to first fill the house with love, and then fill the cookie jar with fresh-baked favorites from our families' recipes—such as the Ginger Snaps cookies Matt is more than happy to taste-test for me."

Recipes

Ginger Snaps

3/4 cup shortening
1 cup sugar
1/4 cup light molasses
1 egg
2 cups flour
2 teaspoons baking soda
1 teaspoon cinnamon
1 teaspoon cloves
1 teaspoon ginger
1/4 teaspoon salt

Cream shortening and sugar. Add egg and molasses, beat well. Stir dry ingredients together and mix well. Shape into 1-1/2" balls, dip in sugar. Place 2-inches apart on ungreased baking sheet. Bake 10–12 minutes at 350º. Makes 48 cookies.

Recipe

Popcorn Balls

2 cups white sugar

1 cup corn syrup

1/2 teaspoon cream
   of tartar

1 tablespoon butter

1/2 teaspoon baking soda

6 quarts popped corn

Combine and cook first 4 ingredients to hardball stage using a candy thermometer. Remove from heat and add baking soda. Pour over popped corn and toss to coat. When cool enough to touch but still warm, butter hands and form balls approximately 3" in diameter. When cool, wrap in cellophane and store in airtight container. Makes 18–24 popcorn balls.

At Halloween, fun times begin with Lynette's special popcorn balls sweetened with candy-corn accents. For an easy, no-bake treat, toss in a handful of cookie ghosts—packaged oval peanut butter cookies dipped in melted white chocolate.

Lynette customized the serving piece by arranging vintage paper Halloween items under the glass top of an antique wooden tray painted black.

Contemporary plates with pumpkins featuring designs from Thimbleberries® fabrics in harvest colors blend beautifully with colorful pottery, a vintage magazine cover, a still-life print, and an antique turkey print.

"The caramel apples— a favorite autumn treat— are made more festive with ribbon and raffia."

Holiday Housewarming

From Thanksgiving to New Year's Day, Lynette takes advantage of Minnesota's long winter season by making every day of the week a holiday housewarming.

From dawn to twilight and throughout the evening, hundreds of twinkling lights, candles, and lamps scattered throughout the two-story house cast a warm glow on everyday activities. In the living room, a harvest tree accompanied by antique Pilgrim and turkey novelty candles sets the scene for a season filled with thanksgiving.

One of Lynette's secrets for combining a beautifully decorated home with working full-time in her own demanding business is to gradually transition from season to season. Harvest pumpkins, dried florals, and the impressive mantel swag welcome a flock of antique turkey candles.

"Painting the walls, windows, and woodwork all in rich shades of cream makes it easy to bring in seasonal color."

One thing that remains
constant in the formal living
room are the black- and -cream
buffalo check upholstered chairs
and couch. Because they provide
the perfect backdrop for Lynette's
variety of seasonal decorating
accents, she never tires of them.

For the several weeks leading up
to Thanksgiving Day, the living
room furniture in this inviting
setting is host to Lynette's Twilight
Garden and Blueberry Patch
quilts in deep shades of rust and
brown, accented with pillows
featuring pumpkin and leaf motifs.

In the dining room, Lynette creates a study in serenity with a still-life painting of fruit and a trio of antique Lipton teapots all in a row. She finds that grouping similar pieces in multiples provides much greater impact than merely displaying them solo.

"For my family, it just wouldn't be Thankgsiving without my antique turkey dishes on the table!"

Nestled on Lynette's Town Square quilt in a corner of the living room, this dollhouse built in 1939 is a nostalgic reminder of most everyone's dream of being home for the holidays. The lid lifts off to reveal a fully furnished house filled with handmade doll furniture.

Lynette created the patchwork stocking with samples of crochet from her grandmother's sewing box. The ribbon reads, "Thanksgiving Eve Ball, Buffalo Lake 1914." (See page 133 for the sweater stocking instructions.)

Recipe

Sugar Cookies

3 cups flour

1 teaspoon baking soda

1 teaspoon cream of tartar

1 cup butter

2 eggs

1 cup sugar

1 teaspoon vanilla or almond flavoring

Stir dry ingredients. Cut in butter with pastry blender. Beat eggs slightly. Add eggs and sugar to flour/butter mixture. Add flavoring, and combine.

Roll dough to 1/8" thickness. Cut out with favorite cookie cutter shapes. Bake at 400° for 8–10 minutes. For a quicker version, dough may also be rolled into 2 logs approximately 2-1/2" in diameter, and refrigerated. Slice into 1/8"-thick slices and bake. Makes 36–48 cookies.

Lynette's Pine Star table runner does double duty as a "place mat for two" when turned sideways on the festive table all dressed up in holiday splendor. (See page 135 for instructions.)

"For a special Christmas-tree table favor, I cut two cookies each using five sizes of star-shaped cutters, then bake the cookies and stack them up—secured with a bit of frosting."

The pine cones on the hooked rug lend design inspiration for Lynette's Whispering Pines quilt topped by her Northern Lights quilt folded at the end of the bed in the guest room. To unify all the interesting angles created by finishing the space over the garage,

Lynette used a popular Early-American stencil— an interesting four seasons sun motif she stenciled on the walls throughout the bedroom.

For the holidays,

the toy barn from

the family room moves

upstairs to join the antique

child's chair, tricycle,

toy sled, and baby buggy

surrounding the tiny

decorated tree tucked

into an alcove

in the bedroom.

Every nook and

cranny gets a

fresh touch at Christmas.

Keeping cozy is

easy in this antique-filled

corner with

Lynette's Up North

quilt ready and

waiting for someone

to "sit for a spell"

in the old chair

by the window.

Caramel Popcorn

2 cups brown sugar

1 cup butter (no substitute)

1/2 cup light corn syrup

1 teaspoon salt

1 teaspoon baking soda

1 tablespoon vanilla

7-1/2 quarts popped corn

Boil butter, brown sugar, corn syrup, and salt in a heavy saucepan for 5 minutes, stirring occasionally. Add baking soda and vanilla; mix thoroughly. Pour over popped corn in large bowl. Mix thoroughly. Place in 2 jelly roll pans or shallow roasting pan. Bake in a 200° oven for 1 hour, stirring every 15 minutes.

"I keep holiday "gifts to go" on hand—popcorn-filled antique quilt-block bags; button-covered heart-shaped boxes; and bundled cookies in cups to go, too!"

Patterns, Swatches & Sources

General Instructions

Hints and Helps for Pressing Strip Sets

When sewing strips of fabric together for strip sets, it is important to press the seam allowances nice and flat, usually to the dark fabric. Be careful not to stretch as you press, causing a "rainbow effect." This will affect the accuracy and shape of the pieces cut

Avoid this rainbow effect

from the strip set. I like to press on the wrong side first and with the strips perpendicular to the ironing board. Then I flip the piece over and press on the right side to prevent little pleats from forming at the seams. Laying the strip set lengthwise on the ironing board seems to encourage the rainbow effect, as shown in diagram.

Borders

Note: Cut borders to the width called for. Always cut border strips a few inches longer than needed, just to be safe. Diagonally piece the border strips together as needed.

Step 1 With pins, mark the center points along all 4 sides of the quilt. For the top and bottom borders measure the quilt from left to right through the middle.

Step 2 Measure and mark the border lengths and center points on the strips cut for the borders before sewing them on.

Step 3 Pin the border strips to the quilt and stitch a 1/4" seam. Press the seam allowances toward the borders. Trim off excess border lengths.

Trim away excess fabric

Step 4 For the side borders, measure your quilt from top to bottom, including the borders just added, to determine the length of the side borders.

Step 5 Measure and mark the side border lengths as you did for the top and bottom borders.

Step 6 Pin and stitch the side border strips in place. Press and trim the border strips even with the borders just added.

Step 7 If your quilt has multiple borders, measure, mark, and sew additional borders to the quilt in the same manner.

Trim away excess fabric

Decorative Stitches

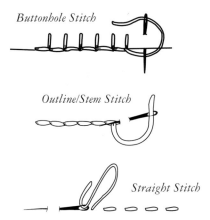

Buttonhole Stitch

Outline/Stem Stitch

Straight Stitch

Finishing the Quilt

Step 1 Remove the selvages from the backing fabric. Sew the long edges together, and press. Trim the backing and batting so they are 2" to 4" larger than the quilt top.

Step 2 Mark the quilt top for quilting. Layer the backing, batting, and quilt top. Baste the 3 layers together and quilt.

Step 3 When quilting is complete, remove basting. Baste all 3 layers together a scant 1/4" from the edge. This hand-basting keeps the layers from shifting and prevents puckers from forming when adding the binding. Trim excess batting and backing fabric even with the edge of the quilt top. Add the binding as shown below.

Binding and Diagonal Piecing

Diagonal Piecing

Stitch diagonally   *Trim to 1/4" seam allowance*   *Press seam open*

Step 1 Diagonally piece the binding strips. Fold the strip in half lengthwise, wrong sides together, and press.

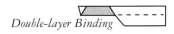

Double-layer Binding

Step 2 Unfold and trim one end at a 45° angle. Turn under the edge 1/4" and press. Refold the strip.

Fold line

Step 3 With raw edges of the binding and quilt top even, stitch with a 3/8" seam allowance, starting 2" from the angled end.

Step 4 Miter the binding at the corners. As you approach a corner of the quilt, stop sewing 3/8" from the corner of the quilt.

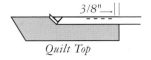

Quilt Top

Step 5 Clip the threads and remove the quilt from under the presser foot.

Step 6 Flip the binding strip up and away from the quilt, then fold the binding down even with the raw edge of the quilt. Begin sewing at the upper edge. Miter all 4 corners in this manner.

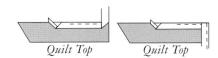

Quilt Top   *Quilt Top*

Step 7 Trim the end of the binding so it can be tucked inside of the beginning binding about 3/8". Finish stitching the seam.

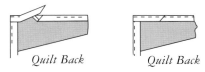

Quilt Back   *Quilt Back*

Step 8 Turn the folded edge of the binding over the raw edges and to the back of the quilt so that the stitching line does not show. Hand-sew the binding in place, folding in the mitered corners as you stitch.

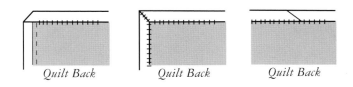

Quilt Back   *Quilt Back*   *Quilt Back*

Homespun Stars Quilt

Shown on page 22

Fabrics and Supplies

31" square

Yardage is based on 42"-wide fabric

45, 11" x 18" pieces (fat eights)
of assorted prints and plaids
for stars and backgrounds

1/3 yard TAN PRINT
for lattice strips

1/8 yard DARK PLAID
for lattice posts

5/8 yard BLUE STRIPE
for border

1/2 yard DARK PLAID
for binding (cut on the bias)

1 yard backing fabric

35" square quilt batting

Star Blocks (Make 9)

Cutting—To make One Star Block

From the Assorted Prints and Plaids:

For the A triangles:
- Cut 1, 3-1/4" square. Cut the square diagonally into quarters, forming 4, A triangles.

For the B squares:
- Cut 4, 2-1/2" squares

For the C triangles:
- Cut 1, 3-1/4" square. Cut the square diagonally into quarters, forming 4, C triangles.

For the D triangles:
- Cut 2, 3-1/4" squares. Cut the squares diagonally into quarters, forming 8, D triangles.

For the E square:
- Cut 1, 2-1/2" square.

Piecing

Step 1 Layer a D triangle on an A triangle. Stitch along the bias edge as shown, being careful not to stretch the triangles, and press. Repeat for 3 more D and A triangles. Make sure you sew with the D triangle on top, and sew along the same bias edge of each triangle set so that your pieced triangle units will all have the D triangle on the same side.

Bias edges

Make 4

Step 2 Layer a D triangle on a C triangle. Stitch along the bias edge as shown, being careful not to stretch the triangles, and press. Repeat for 3 more D and C triangles. Make sure you sew with the D triangle on top, and sew along the same bias edge of each triangle set so that your pieced triangle units will all have the D triangle on the same side.

Bias edges

Make 4

Step 3 Sew the Step 1 and Step 2 triangle units together, and press. At this point the star point unit should measure 2-1/2" square.

Make 4

Step 4 Sew a 2-1/2" B square to both sides of a Step 3 star point unit, and press.

Make 2

Step 5 Sew a star point unit to both sides of a 2-1/2" E square, and press.

Make 1

Step 6 Sew the Step 4 units to both sides of the Step 5 unit, and press. At this point the star block should measure 6-1/2" square.

Step 7 Repeat Steps 1 through 6 to make a total of 9 star blocks.

Make 9

Quilt Center

Cutting

From TAN PRINT:
- Cut 4, 2" x 42" strips. From these strips cut: 24, 2" x 6-1/2" lattice strips.

From DARK PLAID:
- Cut 1, 2" x 42" strip. From this strip cut: 16, 2" squares for lattice posts.

Assembling the Quilt Center

Step 1   Sew together 3 star blocks and 4, 2" x 6-1/2" TAN lattice strips, and press.

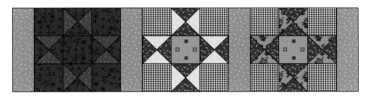

Make 3 block rows

Step 2   Sew together 3, 2" x 6-1/2" TAN lattice strips and 4, 2" DARK PLAID lattice posts, and press.

Make 4 lattice strips

Step 3   Referring to the quilt diagram, sew together the Step 1 block rows and the Step 2 lattice strips, press.

Border

Note: The yardage given allows for the border strips to be cut on the crosswise grain.

Cutting

From BLUE STRIPE:
- Cut 4, 4" x 42" border strips.

Attaching the Border

To attach the 4" wide BLUE STRIPE border strips to the quilt, refer to page 110 for Border Instructions.

Putting It All Together

Trim the backing and batting so they are 4" larger than the quilt top. Refer to Finishing the Quilt on page 111 for complete instructions.

Binding

Cutting

From DARK PLAID:
- Cut enough 2-3/4" wide bias strips to make a 140" long strip.

Sew the binding to the quilt using a 3/8" seam allowance. This measurement will produce a 1/2"-wide finished double binding. Refer to page 111 for Binding and Diagonal Piecing Instructions.

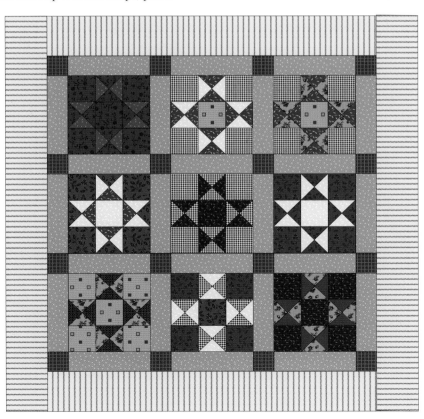

"Beaner" Bunny

Shown on page 23

Fabrics and Supplies

10" x 15" bonded cotton batting or any tightly woven fabric such as cotton calicoes, fine wools, etc. for body

4" x 5" scrap of fabric for vest

4" x 5" fusible web

1 skein embroidery floss
for bunny details;
eyes, nose, whiskers, buttons, etc.

1 skein #8 perle cotton
or embroidery floss
for buttonhole-edge stitching

3/4 cup dried navy beans

Optional: a decorative button
for flower on vest

Construction

Trace bunny and vest patterns onto template material or paper.

Carefully cut out (2) bunny shapes: (1) front and (1) back.

Transfer markings onto bunny front for ears, eyes, nose, whiskers, buttons and shirt (the "v's" above and below button markings).

Iron 4" x 5" piece of fusible web onto vest fabric following manufacturer's instructions. Place vest pattern face down on paper side of prepared fabric and trace (1) vest piece. Flip pattern piece and trace (1) vest piece face up. This will give you a right and left vest piece. Cut and remove paper. Position vest pieces on bunny front. Press in place. Using a buttonhole stitch and either floss or perle cotton, stitch vest to bunny at cuff, neck, front, and bottom of vest.

Sew button on vest with stem and leaf detail using an outline/stem stitch and 3 strands of floss.

Stitch details of bunny front using an outline/stem stitch and 3 strands of floss, stitch the ear detail and shirt markings.

With 3 strands of floss, satin-stitch the nose.

With 3 strands of floss, stitch 2 French Knots for eyes.

With 3 strands of floss, straight-stitch the whiskers and small "x's" for buttons.

With wrong sides together, pin outer edges of bunny together. Start stitching near the bottom and stitch around outside edge with a nice even buttonhole stitch about 1/8" deep. Leave a small opening at bottom, add beans and continue stitching to complete.

"Beaner" will plop down anywhere and look right at home.

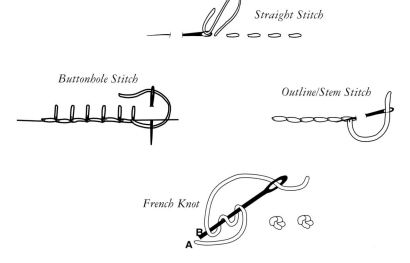

Straight Stitch

Buttonhole Stitch

Outline/Stem Stitch

French Knot

Vest
*Cut 1 and
Cut 1
Reversed*

Neck

Bottom

Bunny
Cut 2

Pillow Cover Border Bloom

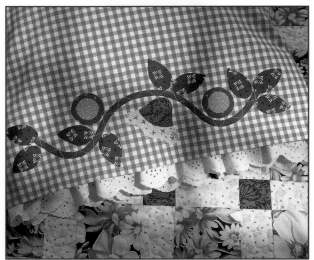

Shown on page 33

Fabric and Supplies

20-1/2" x 27"

Yardage is based on 42"-wide fabric

**1-1/4 yards ROSE CHECK
for pillow cover**

*(This measurement allows for the appliquéd
pillow cover to be layered over a purchased eyelet
ruffle-edged pillowcase. If not layering, check the
measurement of your pillow so that the pillow covering
will completely cover the pillow, allowing a 6" extension.)*

**14" x 20" rectangle GREEN PLAID
for vine appliqué**

**Scraps of assorted prints
for appliqués**

**1/8 yard paper-backed
fusible web for appliqués**

Standard bed pillow form

**Optional: #8 perle cotton
or embroidery floss
for decorative stitching**

Assemble the Pillow Cover

Step 1 Measure the distance around the middle of your pillow form, and add 1" to the measurement to allow for a 1/2" seam allowance. Measure the length of your pillow form, and add 13" to the measurement to allow for a 1/2" seam allowance at one end and a hem at the other end.

Step 2 Cut a ROSE CHECK rectangle according to the measurements determined in Step 1.

Step 3 Turn one long edge under 1/2", and press. Turn the same edge under 6", and press. Topstitch in place to finish the hem.

Step 4 With right sides together, fold the hemmed rectangle in half and sew the side raw edges together using a 1/2" seam allowance. Turn the pillow cover right side out, and press.

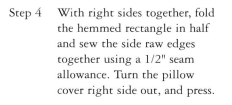

Appliqué the Pillow Cover

Cutting

From GREEN PLAID:
• Cut 1, 1-3/8" x 20" bias strip for the vine

Appliqué the Vine

Step 1 Fold the GREEN PLAID bias strip in half lengthwise with wrong sides together, and press. To keep the raw edges aligned, stitch a scant 1/4" away from the edges. Fold the strip in half again so the raw edges are hidden by the first folded edge, and press.

Step 2 Position the GREEN PLAID vine on the hemmed end of the pillow cover, using the Placement Guide. The vine on the pillow shown was machine-appliquéd using invisible nylon thread and a zigzag stitch. You could also hand appliqué the vine in place.

Fusible Web Appliqué

Step 1 Trace the appliqué shapes on the paper side of the fusible web, leaving 1/2" between each shape. Cut the shapes apart, leaving a small margin beyond the drawn lines.

Step 2 Following the manufacturer's instructions, apply the fusible web shapes to the wrong side of the fabrics chosen for the appliqués. Let the fabrics cool and cut on the traced line. Peel away the paper backing from the fusible web.

Step 3 Referring to the pillow cover Placement Guide, position the appliqué shapes on the pillow cover, and fuse in place.

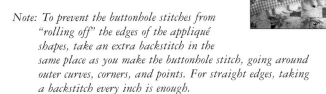

Optional: Buttonhole stitch around the shapes using perle cotton or 3 strands of embroidery floss. The Decorative Stitch diagram is on page 111.

Note: To prevent the buttonhole stitches from "rolling off" the edges of the appliqué shapes, take an extra backstitch in the same place as you make the buttonhole stitch, going around outer curves, corners, and points. For straight edges, taking a backstitch every inch is enough.

2 Flower Circles
Trace 2 of each circle onto fusible web

2-piece Flower
Trace 1 of each piece onto fusible web

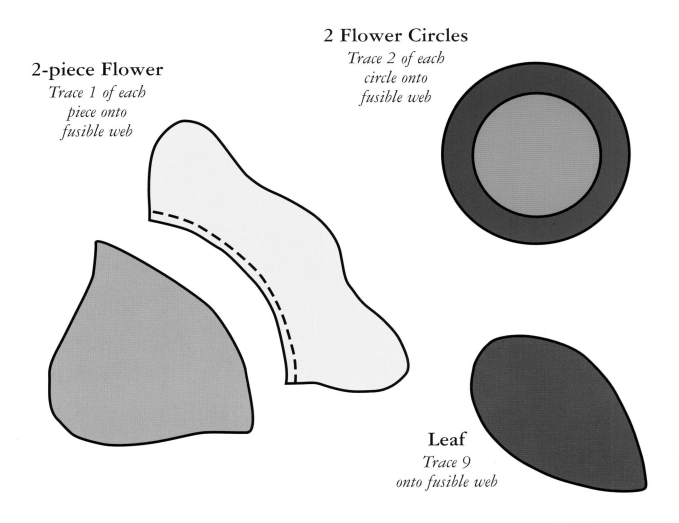

Leaf
Trace 9 onto fusible web

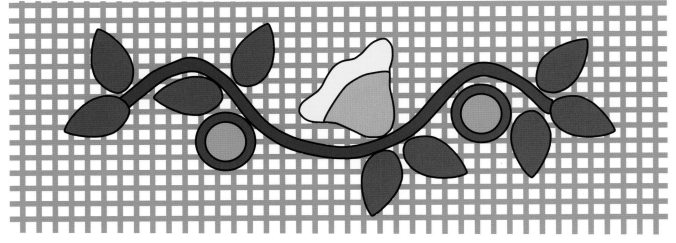

Placement Guide

Shown on page 46

Fabric and Supplies
43" x 53"
Yardage is based on 42"-wide fabric

25 yards of assorted fabrics

Crochet hook size N

*These instructions have been
verbally passed on for years from
generation to generation—*

*Since all fabrics vary as does the
tension of each person's stitches,
it is necessary to increase as needed
to prevent the rug from cupping.*

*The ultimate goal is to have a nice
flat rug without waves or ripples.
Practice definitely makes each rug
better then the first!*

Oval Crocheted Rug

Preparing the Fabric Strips

Step 1   Cut the fabric into 1-1/4" x 42" inch strips.

Step 2   Sew the strips together securely end to end.

Step 3   Fold the strips in half lengthwise, wrong sides together, and roll into several balls, each about 4" in diameter.

Crocheting the Rug

Step 1   Loosely ch 18 sts

Step 2   To turn, sc 2 sts in 2nd ch from last st

Step 3   Loosely sc in each ch st along strip up to the last st

Step 4   In last ch st, loosely sc 3 sts

Step 5   Loosely sc along other side of chain

Step 6   In last ch st, sc 2 st, in the next 2 sts, sc 2 st (6 sts)

Step 7   Continue sc, increase at the ends as needed. Repeat the same increase at the opposite end. Never increase at the sides.

Step 8   When the rug is desired size, hide the loose strip ends in the backside of the rug. Use a smaller crochet hook to work the strips into the stitches.

Making and Attaching the Fringe

Step 1   Cut 1-1/4" x 11" strips from the assorted fabrics.

Step 2   Fold each strip in half lengthwise and then in half crosswise. Using the crochet hook, pull the folded end through one outer stitch of the rug. Slip the free ends of the strip through the loop that was formed and pull to tighten. Repeat for each outer stitch.

Shown on page 37

Fabric and Supplies

89" x 107"
Yardage is based on 42"-wide fabric

2-3/4 yards LARGE BEIGE PRINT
for block centers OR

5-1/2 yards LARGE BEIGE FLORAL
This extra yardage will allow the large
floral design to be centered in each block.

1-1/4 yards SMALL BEIGE FLORAL
for triangle-pieced squares

1 yard GREEN PRINT #1
for triangle-pieced squares

1-1/8 yards GOLD PRINT
for triangle-pieced squares
and middle border

2-5/8 yards BLUE PRINT #1
for pieced block and outer border

1/2 yard BLUE PRINT #2
for pieced block

1/2 yard ROSE PRINT for pieced block

2-1/8 yards GREEN PRINT #2
for lattice and inner border

1 yard GOLD PRINT for binding

8-1/4 yards backing fabric

93" x 111" quilt batting

Flower Bed Quilt

Pieced Blocks (Make 80)

Cutting

From LARGE BEIGE PRINT:
- Cut 14, 6-1/2" x 42" strips.
  From these strips cut: 80, 6-1/2" squares.

OR

From LARGE BEIGE FLORAL:
- Cut 80, 6-1/2" squares, taking care to center a large floral design in the center of each square.

From SMALL BEIGE FLORAL:
- Cut 12, 2-7/8" x 42" strips.

From GREEN PRINT #1:
- Cut 9, 2-7/8" x 42" strips.

From GOLD PRINT:
- Cut 3, 2-7/8" x 42" strips.

From BLUE PRINT #1, BLUE PRINT #2, and ROSE PRINT:
- Cut 5, 2-1/2" x 42" strips from each fabric.

Piecing

Step 1 Sew a BLUE PRINT #1, BLUE PRINT #2, and ROSE PRINT strip together, and press. Repeat to make a total of 5 strip sets. Crosscut the strip sets into segments.

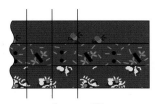

Crosscut 80, 2-1/2" wide segments

Step 2 Layer the 2-7/8" x 42" GREEN PRINT and SMALL BEIGE FLORAL strips together in pairs. Press together, but do not sew. Cut the layered strips into squares.

Crosscut 120, 2-7/8" wide segments

Step 3 Cut the layered squares in half diagonally. Stitch 1/4" from the diagonal edge of each pair of triangles, and press. At this point each triangle-pieced square should measure 2-1/2" square.

Make 240, 2-1/2" triangle-pieced squares

Step 4 Sew 3 GREEN/BEIGE FLORAL triangle-pieced squares together. Repeat to make 80 units.

Make 80

Step 5 Layer the 2-7/8" x 42" GOLD and SMALL BEIGE FLORAL strips together in pairs. Press together, but do not sew. Cut the layered strips into squares.

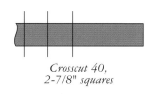

Crosscut 40, 2-7/8" squares

Step 6 Cut the layered squares in half diagonally. Stitch 1/4" from the diagonal edge of each pair of triangles, and press. At this point each triangle-pieced square should measure 2-1/2" square.

Make 80, 2-1/2" triangle-pieced squares

Step 7 Sew a GOLD/BEIGE triangle-pieced square to the right-hand side of each GREEN/BEIGE triangle-pieced square unit. Press the seam allowances toward the GOLD/BEIGE triangle-pieced square.

Make 80

Step 8 Referring to the block diagram, sew the Step 1 segments to the right-hand side of the 6-1/2" LARGE BEIGE FLORAL square. Press the seam allowance toward the FLORAL square. Sew the Step 7 segments to the bottom of the FLORAL square, and press. At this point the blocks should measure 8-1/2" square.

Make 80

Quilt Center

Cutting

From GREEN PRINT #2:
- Cut 18, 1-1/2" x 42" strips. From these strips cut: 72, 1-1/2" x 8-1/2" lattice pieces.
- Cut 27, 1-1/2" x 42" strips for vertical lattice strips and the inner border.

Assembling the Quilt Center

Step 1 Sew 9, 1-1/2" x 8-1/2" GREEN lattice pieces and 10 blocks together for each vertical row. Press the seam allowances toward the lattice pieces. Make 8 vertical block rows.

Step 2 Piece the remaining 1-1/2" x 42" GREEN strips together. Measure the length of the block rows, and trim 7 GREEN vertical lattice strips to this length.

Step 3 Sew the lattice strips and block rows together. Press the seam allowances toward the lattice strips.

Step 4 To attach the GREEN PRINT #2 inner border strips to the quilt, refer to page 110 for Border Instructions.

Middle and Outer Borders

Note: The yardage given allows for the border strips to be cut on the crosswise grain. Diagonally piece the strips as needed, referring to page 111 for Diagonal Piecing Instructions.

Cutting

From GOLD PRINT:
- Cut 9, 2-1/2" x 42" strips for the middle border.

From BLUE PRINT #1:
- Cut 11, 6-1/2 x 42" strips for the outer border.

Attaching the Borders

Step 1 To attach the 2-1/2"-wide GOLD middle border, refer to General Instructions on page 110 for Border Instructions.

Step 2 To attach the 6-1/2"-wide BLUE outer border, refer to General Instructions on page 110 for Border Instructions.

Putting It All Together

Cut the 8-1/4 yard length of backing fabric into thirds crosswise to form 3, 2-3/4-yard lengths. Refer to Finishing the Quilt on page 111 for complete instructions.

Binding
Cutting
From GOLD PRINT:

- Cut 11, 2-3/4" x 42" strips. Sew the binding to the quilt using a 3/8" seam allowance. This measurement will produce a 1/2" wide finished double binding. Refer to page 111 for Binding and Diagonal Piecing Instructions.

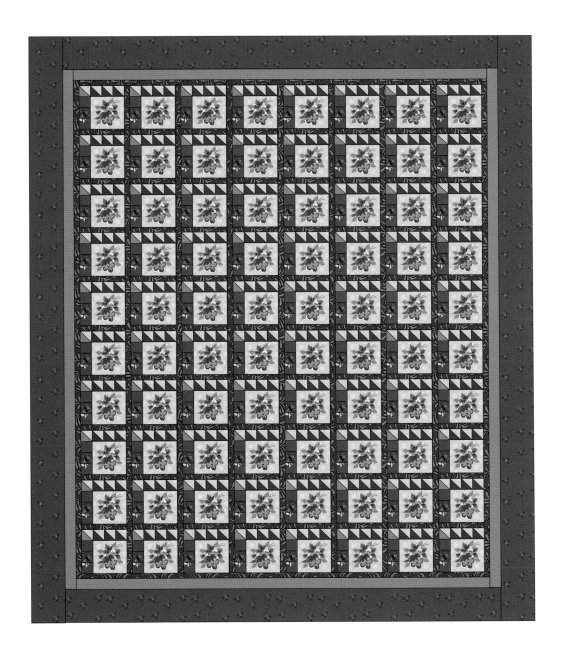

Chair Back Cover

Shown on page 58

Fabric and Supplies

Chair back cover instructions are for bistro-style flat back chair. Alter the yardage and cutting sizes as necessary for a different size chair.

Yardage is based on 42"-wide fabric

3/4 yard BEIGE PRINT for chair back/ties

1/4 yard PINK PLAID
for ruffle and watermelon appliqué

Scraps of GREEN and BROWN PRINTS
for appliqués

1/8 yard paper-backed
fusible web for appliqués

Chair Back Cover

Cutting

From BEIGE PRINT:
- Cut 1, 19" x 35" rectangle.
- Cut 2, 3" x 42" strips. From these strips cut: 4, 3" x 13" strips.

From PINK PLAID:
- Cut 1, 5-1/2" x 36" strip
- Cut 1, 6" square to be used for appliqué

Assemble the Chair Back Cover

Step 1   With right sides together, fold the BEIGE rectangle in half crosswise. Stitch together along the 19" side to form a tube, and press. At this point the rectangle should measure 17-1/2" x 19".

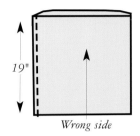

19"

Wrong side

Step 2   With wrong sides together, fold the rectangle in half lengthwise, and press. At this point the rectangle should measure 9-1/2" x 17". Find the center point along the raw edges and mark it with a safety pin.

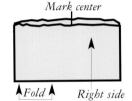

Mark center

Fold   *Right side*

Appliqué the Chair Back Cover

Step 1   To appliqué the chair back cover, trace the appliqué shapes on the paper side of the fusible web, leaving 1/2" between each shape. Cut the shapes apart, leaving a small margin beyond the drawn lines.

Watermelon
*Trace 1
onto fusible web*

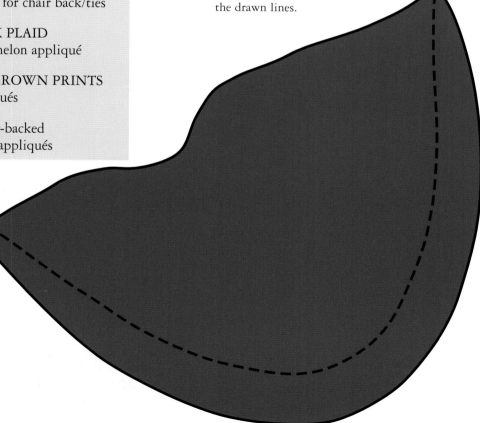

Step 2 Following the manufacturer's instructions, apply the fusible web shapes to the wrong side of the fabrics chosen for the appliqués. Let the fabrics cool and cut on the traced line. Peel away the paper backing from the fusible web.

Step 3 Referring to the project diagram, position and fuse the watermelon shape on the chair back, followed by the rind, and the seeds.

Step 4 Machine appliqué with matching or contrasting thread. These shapes could be buttonhole stitched using perle cotton or embroidery floss. Turn the chair back inside out to attach the ruffle.

Attach the Ruffle

Step 1 To make the ruffle, fold the 2 short ends of the 5-1/2" x 36" PINK PLAID strip in half, right sides together. Stitch across the ends and clip the corners. Turn the ends right sides out, fold the strip in half lengthwise, and press.

Step 2 Divide the strip in half crosswise, and mark the center point with a safety pin.

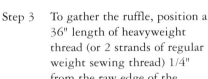

▲*Fold*▲

Step 3 To gather the ruffle, position a 36" length of heavyweight thread (or 2 strands of regular weight sewing thread) 1/4" from the raw edge of the folded ruffle strip.

Secure

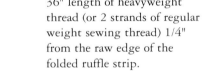

Note: Secure one end of the heavy thread by stitching across it. Then zigzag stitch over the thread the entire length of the ruffle strip, taking care not to sew through the thread.

Step 4 With right sides together, insert the ruffle into the BEIGE rectangle, aligning the raw edges. Match the side edges and the center points, pin the ruffle in place. The ruffle will be inside of the chair back at this point.

Step 5 Gently pull the gathering stitches until the ruffle fits the top edge of the chair back cover. Stitch the ruffle in place. Turn the chair back cover right side out.

Attaching the Ties

Step 1 To make a tie, fold a 3" x 13" BEIGE strip in half lengthwise, with right sides together, and finger press.

Step 2 Cut one end of the tie at a 45° angle. Stitch 1/4" from the cut edges, leaving the end open.

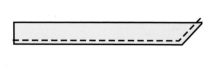

Step 3 Clip the corners, turn the tie right side out, and press, taking care to see that the corner angles are sharp and even. Make 4 ties.

Step 4 Insert the raw edges of the ties 1/2" to the inside of each side of the lower edge of the chair back, taking care to space them evenly. Stitch the ties in place and topstitch around the lower edge of the chair back.

Rind
Trace 1
onto fusible web

Seed
Trace 3 onto fusible web

Appliquéd Tea Towels

Shown on page 76

Fabrics and Supplies

Yardage is based on 42"-wide fabric

Purchased tea towel

Scraps of assorted prints for appliqués

1/8 yard paper-backed
fusible web for appliqués

Fusible Web Appliqué

Step 1   Trace the appliqué shapes on the paper side of the fusible web, leaving 1/2" between each shape. Cut the shapes apart, leaving a small margin beyond the drawn lines.

Step 2   Following the manufacturer's instructions, apply the fusible web shapes to the wrong side of the fabrics chosen for the appliqués. Let the fabrics cool and cut on the traced line. Peel away the paper backing from the fusible web.

Step 3   Referring to the photograph, position the appliqué shapes on the tea towel, and fuse in place.

Step 4   The tea towels shown were machine-appliquéd using matching thread and a zigzag stitch.

Optional: Buttonhole stitch around the shapes using perle cotton or 3 strands of embroidery floss. The Decorative Stitch diagram is found on page 111.

Note: *To prevent the buttonhole stitches from "rolling off" the edges of the appliqué shapes, take an extra backstitch in the same place as you make the buttonhole stitch, going around outer curves, corners, and points. For straight edges, taking a backstitch every inch is enough.*

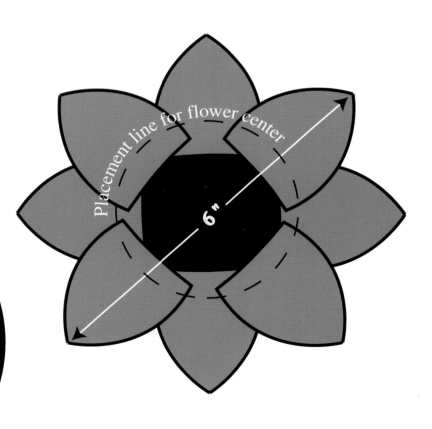

Placement line for flower center

6"

Sunflower Petal
Trace 8 onto fusible web

Sunflower Center
Trace 1 onto fusible web

Leaf
*Trace 1 onto
fusible web*

Leaf
*Trace 1 onto
fusible web*

*Note: These diagrams are
reversed for tracing purposes.*

Stem
*Trace 1 onto
fusible web*

Leaf
*Trace 1 onto
fusible web*

Pumpkin
*Trace 1 of each
pumpkin shape
onto fusible web*

Wool Pumpkin Picture

Shown on page 75

Fabric and Supplies

Yardage is based on 42"-wide fabric

Piece of wool to fit frame
for background

Scraps of assorted wools
for appliqués

#8 Tan and Black
perle cotton or embroidery floss
for decorative stitches

Template material

Appliqué the Pumpkin Picture

Step 1 Trace the appliqué shapes onto the template material and cut out. Using the templates, trace each shape onto the wool fabrics, and cut out.

Step 2 Position the wool shapes on the wool background piece, and appliqué in place with the buttonhole stitch and black perle cotton or 3 strands of embroidery floss. Stem-stitch the leaf veins with black perle cotton or 3 strands of embroidery floss. Stem-stitch the tendrils with tan perle cotton or 3 strands of embroidery floss. Straight stitch the pumpkin sections with black perle cotton or 3 strands of embroidery floss. The decorative stitch diagrams can be found on page 111.

Step 3 We suggest that you take your appliquéd pumpkin picture and frame to a good frame shop to have them do the assembly. The piece shown is not covered with glass.

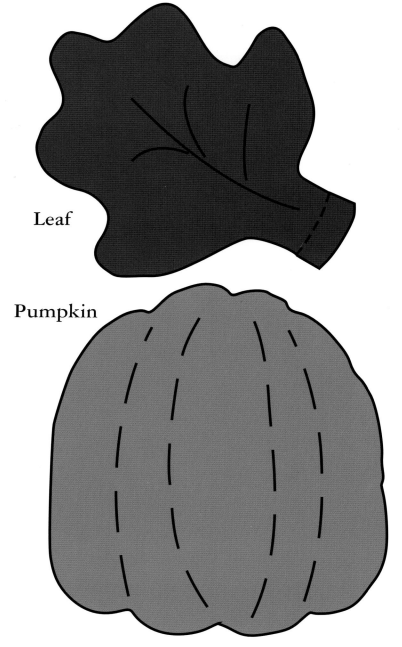

Leaf

Pumpkin

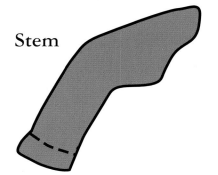

Stem

Pumpkins for Sale

Shown on page 78

Fabric and Supplies

25" square

Yardage is based on 42"-wide fabric

1/8 yard GREEN PRINT #1
for one leaf block and pumpkin stems

1/8 yard each of 6 assorted prints
for leaf blocks (GREEN, CHESTNUT, and RED)

3/8 yard BEIGE PRINT
for background and sawtooth border

4-1/2" x 5-1/2" rectangle
ORANGE PRINT #1 for small pumpkin

1/8 yard ORANGE PRINT #2
for large pumpkin

1/8 yard BROWN PRINT #1 for inner border

1/4 yard BROWN PRINT #2
for sawtooth border and narrow middle border

1/2 yard GREEN PRINT #2
for wide middle border and outer border

3/8 yard ORANGE PRINT #1 for binding

3/4 yard backing fabric

27" square quilt batting

Leaf A (Make 3)

Cutting

From GREEN PRINT #1, one CHESTNUT PRINT, and one RED PRINT:
- Cut 1, 1-1/2" x 3-1/2" rectangle each.
- Cut 1, 1-1/2" x 2-1/2" rectangle each.
- Cut 2, 1-1/2" squares each.
- Cut 1, 3/4" x 2-1/2" strip each.

From BEIGE PRINT:
- Cut 3, 1-3/4" squares.
  Cut the squares in half diagonally for a total of 6 triangles.
- Cut 3, 1-1/2" x 2-1/2" rectangles.
- Cut 9, 1-1/2" squares.

Piecing

Step 1   Position a 1-1/2" GREEN #1 square on the corner of a 1-1/2" x 2-1/2" BEIGE rectangle. Draw a diagonal line on the GREEN square, and stitch on the line. Trim the seam allowance to 1/4", and press. Repeat this process at the opposite corner of the BEIGE rectangle. Sew a 1-1/2" BEIGE square to the right-hand side of this unit, and press.

Step 2   Position a 1-1/2" BEIGE square on the corner of the 1-1/2" x 3-1/2" GREEN #1 rectangle. Draw a diagonal line on the square and stitch on the line. Trim the seam allowance to 1/4", and press.

Step 3   Position a 1-1/2" BEIGE square on the corner of the 1-1/2" x 2-1/2" GREEN #1 rectangle. Draw a diagonal line on the square and stitch on the line. Trim the seam allowance to 1/4", and press.

Step 4   To make the GREEN #1 stem unit, center a 1-3/4" BEIGE triangle on the 3/4" x 2-1/2" GREEN strip, as shown. Stitch a 1/4" seam, trim and press. Repeat on the other side of the GREEN strip. Press the seam allowances toward the stem. Trim the ends of the GREEN stem. At this point the stem unit should measure 1-1/2" square. Sew the Step 3 unit to the right-hand side of the stem unit, and press.

Step 5   Referring to the block diagram, sew together the units from Step 1, 2, and 4, and press. At this point Leaf A should measure 3-1/2" square.

Step 6   For the CHESTNUT and RED PRINT Leaf A blocks, repeat Steps 1 through 5.

Leaf B (Make 4)

Cutting

From 2 GREEN PRINTS, one CHESTNUT PRINT, and one RED PRINT:
- Cut 1, 1-7/8" square each.
- Cut 1, 1-1/2" x 3-1/2" rectangle each.
- Cut 1, 1-1/2" x 2-1/2" rectangle each.
- Cut 1, 1-1/2" square each.
- Cut 1, 3/4" x 2-1/2" strip each.

From BEIGE PRINT:
- Cut 4, 1-7/8" squares.
- Cut 4, 1-3/4" squares. Cut the squares in half diagonally for a total of 8 triangles.
- Cut 8, 1-1/2" squares

Piecing

Step 1   Layer together a 1-7/8" BEIGE and a GREEN square. Cut the layered square in half diagonally. Stitch 1/4" from the diagonal edge of each pair of triangles, and press. Sew the triangle-pieced squares together, then add a 1-1/2" GREEN square to the right-hand side of this unit, and press

Make 2, 1-1/2" triangle-pieced squares

Step 2   Position a 1-1/2" BEIGE square on the corner of a 1-1/2" x 3-1/2" GREEN rectangle. Draw a diagonal line on the square; stitch on the line. Trim the seam allowance to 1/4"; press.

Step 3   Position a 1-1/2" BEIGE square on the corner of a 1-1/2" x 2-1/2" GREEN rectangle. Draw a diagonal line on the square and stitch on the line. Trim the seam allowance to 1/4" and press.

Step 4   To make the GREEN stem unit, refer to Leaf A, Step 4. Sew the Step 3 unit to the right-hand side of the stem unit, and press.

Step 5   Referring to the block diagram, sew together the units from Step 1, 2, and 4, and press. At this point Leaf B should measure 3-1/2" square.

Step 6   For the remaining GREEN, CHESTNUT, and RED PRINT Leaf B blocks, repeat Steps 1 through 5.

Pumpkins

Cutting

From ORANGE PRINT #1:
- Cut 1, 4-1/2" x 5-1/2" rectangle.

From ORANGE PRINT #2:
- Cut 1, 2-3/8" x 2-7/8" rectangle.
- Cut 1, 2-1/2" x 7-1/2" rectangle.
- Cut 1, 2-1/2" square.
- Cut 1, 1-1/2" x 6-1/2" rectangle.
- Cut 3, 1-1/2" squares.

From BEIGE PRINT:
- Cut 1, 2-7/8" square.
- Cut 1, 2-1/2" square.
- Cut 5, 1-1/2" squares.

From GREEN PRINT #1:
- Cut 1, 1-1/2" x 2-1/2" rectangle.
- Cut 1, 1-1/2" square.
- Cut 1, 1" x 2-7/8" rectangle.
- Cut 1, 1" square.

Piecing

Step 1   Position 3, 1-1/2" ORANGE PRINT #2 squares and 1, 1-1/2" BEIGE square on the corners of the 4-1/2" x 5-1/2" ORANGE PRINT #1 rectangle, as shown. Draw a diagonal line on the squares and stitch on these lines. Trim the seam allowances to 1/4", and press.

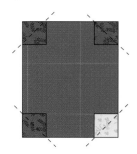

Step 2   Position 2, 1-1/2" BEIGE squares on the corners of the 1-1/2" x 6-1/2" ORANGE PRINT #2 rectangle, as shown. Draw diagonal lines on the squares and stitch on these lines. Trim the seam allowances to 1/4", and press. Set this unit aside to be used in the Quilt Center section.

Step 3 Position a 1-1/2" BEIGE square on the corner of the 2-1/2" x 7-1/2" ORANGE PRINT #2 rectangle. Draw a diagonal line on the BEIGE square and stitch on the line. Trim the seam allowance to 1/4", and press.

Step 4 Position a 1-1/2" GREEN PRINT #1 square on the corner of the 2-1/2" ORANGE PRINT #2 square. Draw a diagonal line on the GREEN square and stitch on the line.

Make 1

Trim the seam allowance to 1/4", and press. Repeat at the opposite corner of the ORANGE square with the 1" GREEN #1 square, as shown.

Step 5 Sew the 1" x 2-7/8" GREEN #1 rectangle to the left-hand side of the 2-3/8" x 2-7/8" ORANGE PRINT #2 rectangle, and press. Layer the 2-7/8" BEIGE square on this unit. Cut the layered square in half diagonally. Stitch a 1/4" seam along the diagonal edge of the lower triangle, as shown, and press. Sew this unit to the right-hand side of the Step 4 unit, and press.

Make 1

Make 1

Step 6 Position a 1-1/2" BEIGE square on the corner of the 1-1/2" x 2-1/2" GREEN #1 rectangle. Draw a diagonal line on the BEIGE square and stitch on the line. Trim the seam allowance to 1/4", and press. Sew this unit to the right-hand side of the 2-1/2" BEIGE square as shown, and press

Make 1

Quilt Center

Cutting

From BEIGE PRINT:
- Cut 4, 2-1/2" x 3-1/2" rectangles.
- Cut 1, 1-1/2" x 3-1/2" rectangle.

Quilt Center Assembly

Referring to the quilt assembly diagram, lay out the leaf blocks, pumpkin sections, and BEIGE rectangles. For the left-hand section, sew the pieces together in horizontal rows, and press. Sew the rows together, and press. For the right-hand section, sew the pieces together in vertical rows, and press. Sew the sections together, and press. At this point the quilt center should measure 12-1/2" square.

Borders

Note: The yardage given allows for the border strips to be cut on the crosswise grain. Diagonally piece the strips as needed, referring to page 111 for Diagonal Piecing Instructions.

Cutting

From BROWN PRINT #1:
- Cut 2, 1-1/2" x 42" strips for the inner border.

From BROWN PRINT #2:
- Cut 2, 1-7/8" x 42" strips for the sawtooth border.
- Cut 3, 1" x 42" strips for narrow middle border.

From BEIGE PRINT:
- Cut 2, 1-7/8" x 42" strips for the sawtooth border.
- Cut 4, 1-1/2" squares for the sawtooth corner squares.

From GREEN PRINT #2:
- Cut 5, 2-1/2" x 42" strips for the wide middle border and outer border.

Attaching the Borders

Step 1   To attach the 1-1/2" wide BROWN PRINT #1 inner border strips, refer to page 110 for Border Instructions.

Step 2   To make the sawtooth border, layer the 1-7/8" x 42" BROWN PRINT #2 and BEIGE strips together in pairs. Press them together, but do not sew. Cut the layered strips into squares.

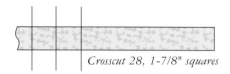

Crosscut 28, 1-7/8" squares

Step 3   Cut the layered squares in half diagonally. Stitch 1/4" from the diagonal edge of each pair of triangles, and press. At this point each triangle-pieced square should measure 1-1/2" square.

Make 56, 1-1/2" triangle-pieced squares

Step 4   Sew 14 triangle-pieced squares together for each sawtooth border strip, and press. Sew 2 of the borders to the top and bottom of the quilt, and press.

Step 5   Add 1-1/2" BEIGE squares to both ends of the remaining sawtooth borders, and press. Sew these borders to the sides of the quilt, and press.

Step 6   To attach the 2-1/2"-wide GREEN PRINT #2 middle border strips, refer to page 110 for Border Instructions.

Step 7   To attach the 1" wide BROWN PRINT #2 narrow middle border strips, refer to page 110 for Border Instructions.

Step 8   To attach the 2-1/2"-wide GREEN PRINT #2 outer border strips, refer to page 110 for Border Instructions.

Putting It All Together

Trim the backing and batting so they are about 2" larger than the quilt top. Refer to Finishing the Quilt on page 111 for complete instructions.

Binding

Cutting

From ORANGE PRINT#1:
- Cut 3, 2-3/4" x 42" strips.

Sew the binding to the quilt using a 3/8" seam allowance. This measurement will produce a 1/2" wide finished double binding. Refer to page 111 for Binding and Diagonal Piecing Instructions.

Harvest Pinwheels

Shown on page 81

Fabric and Supplies

63" square
Yardage is based on 42"-wide fabric

1 yard BROWN PRINT
for pinwheels and sawtooth

1 yard BEIGE PRINT #1
for block background

1/2 yard GREEN PRINT #1 for blocks

3/4 yard GOLD PRINT
for blocks and first inner border

5/8 yard BEIGE PRINT #2 for center square

3/4 yard RED PRINT
for second inner border, lattice,
and narrow outer border

1-1/2 yards GREEN PRINT #2
for third inner border and wide outer border

2/3 yard RED PRINT for binding

4 yards backing fabric

67" square quilt batting

Harvest Blocks (Make 12)

Cutting

From BROWN PRINT:
- Cut 9, 2-7/8" x 42" strips.

From BEIGE PRINT #1:
- Cut 9, 2-7/8" x 42" strips.

From GREEN PRINT #1:
- Cut 6, 2-1/2" x 42" strips. From these strips cut: 48, 2-1/2" x 4-1/2" rectangles.

From GOLD PRINT:
- Cut 6, 2-1/2" x 42" strips. From these strips cut: 96, 2-1/2" squares.

Piecing

Step 1   Layer together the 2-7/8" x 42" BROWN and BEIGE strips in pairs. Press together; do not sew. Cut the layered strips into squares.

Crosscut 120, 2-7/8" layered squares

Step 2   Cut the layered squares in half diagonally. Stitch 1/4" from the diagonal edge of each pair of triangles, and press. At this point each triangle-pieced square should measure 2-1/2"square.

Make 240, 2-1/2" triangle-pieced squares

Step 3   Referring to the diagram, sew triangle-pieced squares together in pairs, and press. Make 24 pairs. Sew the pairs together and press to complete the pinwheel unit. At this point the pinwheel unit should measure 4-1/2" square.

Make 12

Step 4   Sew 2-1/2" x 4-1/2" GREEN rectangles to the top and bottom of the pinwheel unit, and press. Add 2-1/2" GOLD squares to both ends of the remaining 2-1/2" x 4-1/2" GREEN rectangles, and press. Sew these units to the sides of the block, and press. At this point the block should measure 8-1/2" square.

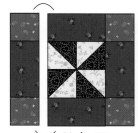

Make 12

Step 5   Sew 4, Step 2 triangle-pieced squares together for each sawtooth border, and press.

Make 48

Step 6   Sew a sawtooth border to the top and bottom of the block, and press. Add a 2-1/2" GOLD square to both ends of the remaining sawtooth borders, and press. Sew a sawtooth border to both sides of the block, and press. At this point the block should measure 12-1/2" square.

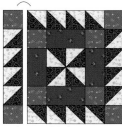

Make 12

Inner Borders

Note: The yardage given allows for the border strips to be cut on the crosswise grain. Diagonally piece the strips as needed, referring to page 111 for Diagonal Piecing Instructions.

Cutting

From BEIGE #2:
- Cut 1, 17-1/2" center square.

From GOLD PRINT:
- Cut 2, 2-1/2" x 42" strips for first inner border.

From RED PRINT:
- Cut 3, 1-1/2" x 42" strips for second inner border.

From GREEN PRINT #2:
- Cut 4, 2-1/2" x 42" strips for third inner border.

Attaching the Inner Border Strips

Step 1   To attach the 2-1/2" wide GOLD inner border strips to the quilt, refer to page 110 for Border Instructions.

Step 2   To attach the 1-1/2" wide RED inner border strips to the quilt, refer to page 110 for Border Instructions.

Step 3   To attach the 2-1/2" wide GREEN PRINT #2 inner border strips to the quilt, refer to page 110 for Border Instructions.

Quilt Center

Cutting

From RED PRINT:
- Cut 4, 1-1/2" x 42" strips.
  From these strips cut:
  12, 1-1/2" x 12-1/2" lattice strips.

Assemble the Quilt Center

Step 1   Sew together 2 blocks and 3, 1-1/2" x 12-1/2" RED lattice strips, and press. Make 2 block rows, and sew them to the top and bottom of the quilt center, and press.

Step 2   Sew together 4 blocks and 3, 1-1/2" x 12-1/2" RED lattice strips, and press. Make 2 block rows and sew them to the sides of the quilt center, and press.

Outer Borders

Note: The yardage given allows for the border strips to be cut on the crosswise grain. Diagonally piece the strips as needed, referring to page 111 for Diagonal Piecing Instructions.

Cutting

From RED PRINT:
- Cut 6, 1-1/2" x 42" narrow outer border strips.

From GREEN PRINT#2:
- Cut 7, 5-1/2" x 42" wide outer border strips.

Attaching the Borders

Step 1   To attach the 1-1/2"-wide RED narrow outer border strips to the quilt, refer to page 110 for Border Instructions.

Step 2   To attach the 5-1/2"-wide GREEN PRINT #2 wide outer border strips to the quilt, refer to page 110 for Border Instructions.

Putting It All Together

Cut the 4 yard length of backing fabric in half crosswise to make 2, 2 yard lengths. Refer to Finishing the Quilt on page 111 for complete instructions.

Binding

Cutting

From RED PRINT:
- Cut 7, 2-3/4" x 42" strips.

Sew the binding to the quilt using a 3/8" seam allowance. This measurement will product a 1/2"-wide finished double binding. Refer to page 111 for Binding and Diagonal Piecing Instructions.

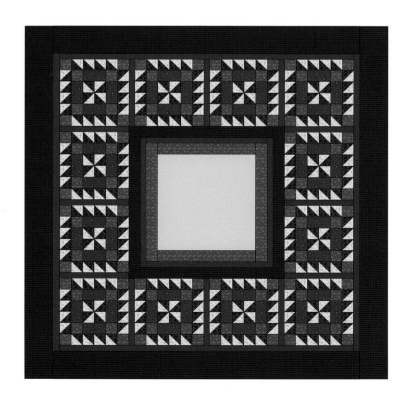

Sweater Stocking

Shown on page 99

Fabric and Supplies

11" long

*Recycle a once-loved sweater,
especially one with interesting cuffs,
bands, yarn, or colors for stocking*

2-ply contrasting yarn
for tree, buttonhole stitching, and hanger

#8 contrasting perle cotton
or embroidery floss
for star and tree base

12, 1/4" pewter bells
for tree ornaments

4, 5/8" pewter bells
for hanger trim

Assemble the Stocking

Step 1   The charming stocking is cut from a once-loved sweater. Position the stocking pattern so the top of the stocking takes advantage of the cuff or bottom band of the sweater. Cut a front and a back piece.

Step 2   Stem-stitch the tree, star, and tree base on the stocking front. Sew the tiny pewter bells to the tips of the tree branches.

Step 3   With wrong sides together, machine-stitch the stocking front and back pieces together using a 3/8" seam allowance and matching thread.

Step 4   An oversized buttonhole stitch decorates the stocking edge using the machine-stitching line as a guide.

Step 5   To make the hanger, cut 2, 5"-long pieces of yarn and thread them through the top corner of the stocking and knot the ends. For a decorative touch, cut 2, 8"-long pieces of yarn and thread them through the top edge of the stocking. Tie a knot close to the stocking. Tie the large bells to the ends of the yarn.

*Decorative Stitches:
Outline/Stem Stitch and Buttonhole
Stitch can be found on page 111.*

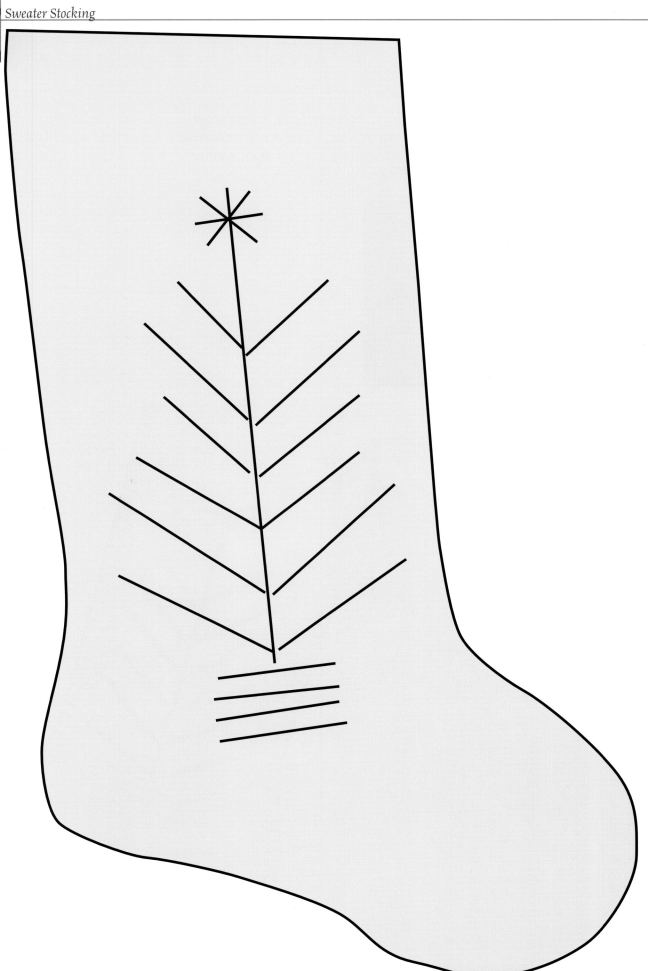

Pine Star Runner

Shown on page 100

Fabrics and Supplies

23" x 57"

Yardage is based on 42"-wide fabric

1/4 yard GREEN PRINT #1
for tree points

1/2 yard BEIGE PRINT for background

5/8 yard GREEN PRINT #2
for trees and border

1/8 yard BROWN PRINT for tree trunks

3/4 yard RED PRINT #1
for star and side and corner triangles

1/2 yard RED PRINT #2 for binding

1-1/2 yards backing fabric

27" x 61" quilt batting

A rotary cutter, mat, and wide clear plastic ruler with 1/8" markings are necessary tools in attaining accuracy.

A 6" x 24" ruler is recommended.

Tree Blocks (Make 2)

Cutting

From the GREEN PRINT #1:
- Cut 1, 2-7/8" x 42" strip.
- Cut 2, 2-1/2" squares.

From the BEIGE PRINT:
- Cut 2, 6" squares.
- Cut 1, 2-7/8 x 42" strip.
- Cut 4, 2-1/2" squares.

From the GREEN PRINT #2:
- Cut 1, 4-1/2" x 42" strip. From this strip cut:
  2, 4-1/2" x 8-1/2" rectangles and 2, 4-1/2" squares.

From the BROWN PRINT:
- Cut 2, 1-3/4" x 11" strips.

Piecing

Step 1 Layer together the 2-7/8" x 42" GREEN PRINT #1 strip and the 2-7/8" x 42" BEIGE strip. Press together, but do not sew. Cut the layered strip into squares.

Crosscut 12, 2-7/8" squares

Step 2 Cut the layered squares in half diagonally. Stitch 1/4" from the diagonal edge of each pair of triangles, and press. At this point each triangle-pieced square should measure 2-1/2" square.

Make 24, 2-1/2" triangle-pieced squares

Step 3 Sew the Step 2 triangle-pieced squares together in pairs, and press. Refer to the diagram for placement of the triangles.

Make 6 Unit A

Make 6 Unit B

Step 4 Sew a Unit A to both ends of a 4-1/2" x 8-1/2" GREEN PRINT #2 rectangle, and press. At this point the unit should measure 4-1/2" x 12-1/2".

Make 2

Step 5 Sew a Unit A to the left-hand side of a 4-1/2" GREEN PRINT #2 square, and press.

Make 2

Step 6 Sew a 2-1/2" BEIGE square to the left-hand side of a Unit B, and press. Sew this unit to the bottom of the Step 5 unit, and press. At this point the unit should measure 6-1/2" square.

Make 2

135

Step 7 Sew the remaining B Units together in pairs, and press. Sew a 2-1/2" GREEN PRINT #1 square to the left-hand side of each unit, and press. Sew a 2-1/2" BEIGE square to the right-hand side of each unit, and press. Sew these units to the top of the Step 4 units, and press. At this point each unit should measure 6-1/2" x 12-1/2".

Make 2

Step 8 Cut the 6" BEIGE squares in half diagonally. Center a BEIGE triangle on the 1-3/4" x 11" BROWN strip. Stitch a 1/4" seam, and press the seam allowance toward the BROWN strip. Center another BEIGE triangle on the BROWN strip, stitch and press. The trunk strip will extend beyond the triangles. Trim the ends of the trunk so that the unit measures 6-1/2" square.

Trim excess

Make 2

Step 9 Sew the Step 8 trunk units to the right-hand side of the Step 6 units, and press.

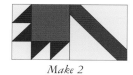

Make 2

Step 10 Sew the Step 9 units to the bottom of the Step 7 units, and press. At this point the blocks should measure 12-1/2" square.

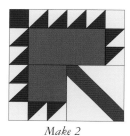

Make 2

Star Block (Make 1)

Cutting

From the RED PRINT #1:
- Cut 1, 4-1/2" square.
- Cut 8, 2-1/2" squares.

From the BEIGE PRINT:
- Cut 2, 2-1/2" x 42" strips. From these strips cut: 2, 2-1/2" x 12-1/2" strips, 2, 2-1/2" x 8-1/2" strips, 4, 2-1/2" x 4-1/2" rectangles, 4, 2-1/2" squares.

Piecing

Step 1 Position a 2-1/2" RED square on the corner of a 2-1/2" x 4-1/2" BEIGE rectangle. Draw a diagonal line on the RED square, and stitch on the line. Trim away

the excess corner fabric, leaving a 1/4" seam allowance, and press. Repeat this process at the opposite corner of the BEIGE rectangle.

    Make 4

Step 2 Sew Step 1 units to the top and bottom of the 4-1/2" RED square, and press. Sew 2-1/2" BEIGE squares to both sides of the remaining Step 1 units, and press. Sew these units to the sides of the block, and press. At this point the block should measure 8-1/2" square.

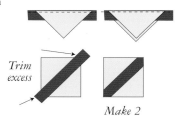

Make 1   *Make 1*

Step 3 Sew 2-1/2" x 8-1/2" BEIGE strips to the top and bottom of the Step 2 star block, and press. Sew 2-1/2" x 12-1/2" BEIGE strips to the sides of the star block, and press. At this point the block should measure 12-1/2" square.

Quilt Center

Note: The side and corner triangles are larger than necessary and will be trimmed before the border is added.

Cutting

From the RED PRINT #1:
- Cut 1, 19" square. Cut the square diagonally into quarters for a total of 4 side triangles.
- Cut 2, 10" squares. Cut the squares in half diagonally for a total of 4 corner triangles.

Assembling the Runner Center

Step 1 Referring to the diagram, sew the tree blocks, star block, and side triangles together in diagonal rows. Press the seam allowances in alternating directions by rows so the seams will fit snugly together with less bulk.

Step 2 Pin the rows at the block intersections, and sew the rows together. Press the seam allowances in one direction.

Step 3 Sew the corner triangles to the runner, and press.

Step 4 Trim away the excess fabric from the side and corner triangles, taking care to allow a 1/4" seam allowance beyond the corners of each block. Refer to Trimming Side and Corner Triangles.

Trimming Side & Corner Triangles

- Begin at a corner by lining up your ruler 1/4" beyond the points of the corners of the blocks as shown. Draw a light line along the edge of the ruler. Repeat this procedure on all four sides of the runner top, lightly marking cutting lines.

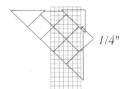

Mark cutting lines lightly 1/4" beyond the points of the corners of the blocks

1/4"

- Check all the corners before you do any cutting. Adjust the cutting lines as needed to ensure square corners.

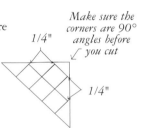

Make sure the corners are 90° angles before you cut

1/4"

1/4"

- When you are certain that everything is as square as it can be, position your ruler over the runner top. Using your marked lines as guides, cut away the excess fabric with your rotary cutter, leaving a 1/4" seam allowance beyond the block corners.

Border

Note: The yardage given allows for the border strips to be cut on the crosswise grain. Diagonally piece the strips as needed, referring to page 111 for Diagonal Piecing Instructions.

Cutting

From the GREEN PRINT #2:
- Cut 4, 3-1/2" x 42" strips for the border.

Attaching the Border

To attach the 3-1/2"-wide GREEN PRINT #2 border strips to the runner, refer to page 110 for Border Instructions.

Putting It All Together

- Cut the 1-1/2 yard length of backing fabric in half crosswise to make 2, 3/4 yard lengths. Refer to Finishing The Quilt on page 111 for complete instructions.

Binding

Cutting

From the RED PRINT #2:
- Cut 4, 2-3/4" x 42" strips.

Sew the binding to the runner using a 3/8" seam allowance. This measurement will produce a 1/2"-wide finished double binding. Refer to page 111 for Binding and Diagonal Piecing Instructions.

SWATCHES TO GO

Lynette has created a palette of coordinating fabric
and color chips that blends perfectly for each season to
transition you through the year in style.

To use this practical system as the basis for your own
country decorating, simply take the following pages with four
seasons of "swatches to go" to your quilt shop or fabric store for
handy reference. The Thimbleberries® fabrics shown here are
some of Lynette's all-time favorites and may or may not be
currently available. However, the unique feature of
Thimbleberries®—especially the Paintbox Collection—is that
you can mix and match fabrics because they blend from collection
to collection. You'll find the basic color palette an easy reference
for selecting seasonal-color fabric for quilts, pillows, and other
decorating accessories. Once you've selected fabrics, then take
these same pages to your paint store to choose complementary
paint colors for windows, walls, and painted furniture and
accessories. With all your basics in place, you can quickly and
confidently transition to another decorating season.

Thanks to Lynette, you can make it beautiful and make it
easy, too. With this unique system of "swatches to go" she
offers you the best of everything for creating four seasons
of your own authentic country decorating.

Spring

Summer

Harvest

Holiday

Spring Swatches to Go

Summer Swatches to Go

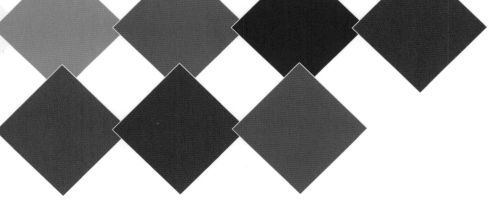

Harvest Swatches to Go

Holiday Swatches to Go

SOURCES

Many of Lynette Jensen's designs for quilts, pillows, and table runners shown in
CLASSIC COUNTRY *as decorative accessories are featured projects available from her Thimbleberries®*
line of books and patterns or from Rodale Books. Please call 800/587-3944 to order a catalog or for
more information on obtaining patterns and instructions for the projects sourced in the gallery below.

THIMBLEBERRIES®